ARE WE SHEEP?

L. J. SLOAN

ISBN: 0615613322
ISBN-13: 9780615613321

I dedicate this book to my two daughters and three grandchildren. Their future and the future of all our loved ones are in our hands. We can accept things as they are today or do something to truly make a change.

FORWARD

The intention of this informational booklet and the series to follow is to awaken the nation and its people to the unjustness and outright incompetence in the past and existing government leadership of the United States of America.

In this series we will discuss the unjustness of hundreds of billions of your dollars. In some cases, trillions of dollars being lost, unaccounted for, wasted, and misspent for the sole benefit of special interest groups. As we stand here in the twenty-first century, we face an unemployment rate equal to that of the Great Depression and the highest American debt ($16 trillion) in our history. I ask you what will it take to get your voice and the nation as a whole heard loud and clear in the back rooms in Washington, DC?

It is time that we (the people of this nation) take back our country and purge the waste of our tax dollars and, most importantly, remove the men and women behind the malfeasance from office. How do we do this? We do it collectively as a united nation with the values and vision our forefathers used in creating the United States of America.

The task of ushering in new political leadership will be explored more fully in an informational booklet that will follow shortly. But for now, we will focus on bringing to light the unjustness being inflicted upon our nation and its people by the leaders in our government, the political elite who believe they are untouchable and a necessity for our government to work.

CONTENT

PART – 1

WHERE WE ARE TODAY

We will start off by covering just a small fraction of the outrageous and wasteful spending that has occurred during the last four years of the existing presidency. But most importantly remember this; where we are today in regards to our deficit and the total lack of accountability to wasteful sending by our appointed leaders in Government did not just occur in the past four years. This booklet is mainly a compilation of writings that illustrate a long history of government financial malfeasance that continues to this very day. It will also show the mindset that occurs when an appointed government official is placed in power in Washington DC. And what transformation takes place when they are exposed to the malignant thoughts of saving his/her place of power at any cost.

As we progress through the book you will see a systemic problem that has been occurring over the past decades. It highlights how all of the wasted Billions of tax dollars have been successfully hidden under the radar in order not to upset the common tax payer. It will also make very clear the needs of our politicians to throw money at special interest groups and home projects in order to maintain the support and financial backing that they crave for.

It is time, that we as a society, concern ourselves with more than being fat, dumb and happy with our SUV, three bedroom home, two or three children and our dog. We need to look beyond our nose, beyond our front yards. We need to recognize how our government officials are stealing our future and the future of our children. It is time we make our politicians look at our nation as more than contented sheep grazing and only concerned about ourselves. We must take back our county and make Washington DC understand that they work for the people of this great country. "We do not work to line their pockets with our tax dollars or to support their special interests groups".

Get ready to have your eyes opened, your blood pressure raised and your frustration threshold challenged:

The U.S. Agency for International Development (U.S. AID) spent $30 million to spur mango production and sales in Pakistan—and failed utterly. The Air Force spent $14 million to switch three radar stations to wind power; poor planning forced cancellation of one turbine and consideration of the same for the other two. The Federal Aviation Administration devoted $6 million to subsidize air service at small, underused airports.

A federal grant for $765,828 went to—I am not making this up; to quote Dave Barry—bring an International House of Pancakes franchise to Washington, D.C. Although the famed "Bridge to

Nowhere" might never be built, Uncle Sam still shelled out $15.3 million in project costs, including a 14-minute promotional video, on top of $50 million already absorbed by the Knik Arm Bridge. The Office of Personnel Management sent $120 million to dead federal employees (actually, they probably did less harm than the live ones!).

The Department of Transportation spent $529.689 to create the fourth visitor center around the 54 mile Talimena Scenic Drive between Oklahoma and Arkansas. A check for $113,277 was cut to help the International Center for the History of Electronic Games to preserve "historic" video games. Washington helpfully gave almost $18 million in foreign aid to China—money effectively borrowed from China. The Department for Housing and Urban Development (HUD) provided a $484,000 grant to build a "Mellow Mushroom Pizza Bakers" restaurant in Texas.

Uncle Sam sent $100,000 to the Washington State Fruit Commission to stage a "celebrity chef fruit promotion road show" in Indonesia. U.S. AID gave $10 million to an arts organization in Pakistan—a country threatened with disintegration—to produce local episodes of Sesame Street. Then there was $150,000 for the American Museum of Magic in Marshall, Michigan. Another HUD grant, this one for $1 million, went to a foreign architectural firm to move its headquarters from Santa Monica to Los Angeles. The federal government cut a check for $550,000 to underwrite a documentary on the impact of rock and roll on the collapse of communism.

The National Institutes of Health (NIH) provided a $702,558 grant for the study of the impact of televisions and gas generators on villages in Vietnam. Hawaii's annual Chocolate Festival collected

$48,700 from Washington. People who didn't own homes, such as children and prisoners, claimed as much as a billion dollars in tax credits for promoting energy efficiency in their homes. The Department of Commerce gave $936,818 to create a web TV soap opera on single moms to spur adoption of broadband.

Michigan received $75,000 to promote Christmas trees and poinsettias. The State Department spent $350,000 to underwrite an arts festival in Venice, Italy. NIH gave the University of Kentucky $175,587 to study the impact of cocaine on the sex drive of Japanese quail. A grant for $2 million went to Washington State's Walter Clore Wine and Culinary Center.

The Department of Agriculture spent $200 million—still not real money in the nation's capital—to promote industry groups, cooperatives, and corporations. The Centers for Disease Control and Prevention (CDC) spent $385,005 to survey what bus riders thought of HIV videos. Maine collected $95,000 to purchase iPads for kindergarteners. The Agency for Health Research and Quality spent more than $1 million to get people to visit its website. The National Science Foundation (NSF) used $200,000 to see what the public thinks of politicians and climate change.

The Federal Highway Administration (FHA) gave $916,567 to underwrite horse-drawn carriage exhibits and survey shipwrecks in Wisconsin. The Veterans Administration spent $221,540 on a conference on disability ratings. NSF spent $300,000 for tourism podcasts in Alaska. The IRS used $862,000 to store unused furniture and equipment. NSF (again!) spent nearly a half million dollars to study whether people trust Tweets from Twitter. U.S. AID devoted $12 million to help the hapless Pakistanis use less energy.

The Oregon Cheese Guild received $50,400 to promote cheese. HUD gave $168 million, still pocket change in Washington, to the federally chartered Neighborhood Reinvestment Corporation, deemed unnecessary and duplicative by the Congressional Budget Office. The Agriculture Department, another multiple offender, spent $73,824 to encourage bed and breakfasts to use local produce. New Hampshire's Museum on the History of Skiing received $86,000.

Fraud and waste in wartime contracting may have cost about $4.4 billion. Now that's real money!

Uncle Sam spent $111,000 to send brewery experts to conduct classes in China. A grant for $24,632 went for the Milwaukee Public Museum to produce a 3-D virtual mummy unwrapping. NSF (won't they ever stop?) provided $149,990 for production of a guppy-to-fish video game. The Department of Agriculture spent $9.49 million on a duplicative program in management of foreign forests which even the White House wants to eliminate. Washington used $697,006 to beautify Las Vegas highways.

The ubiquitous NSF spent $764,825 to study student social networking. The equally wasteful Agriculture Department devoted $171,050 for a farm marketing effort in Vermont. The federal government paid $136,555 so teachers could retrace the steps of Chaucer's Canterbury Tales. The Energy Department's $231 million weatherization program was inefficient, wasteful and duplicative.

U.S. AID underwrote a $1.35 million "entrepreneurship initiative" in Barbados. The Coast Guard spent $24,450 on a float in the Mardi Gras. NSF (yet again!) spent $126,242 on a study of campaign websites. Salt Lake City received $150,000 to renovate a carriage house. The Department of Transportation spent $8.3 million to preserve covered bridges. Wine promotion benefited from $62,000 in federal promotional funds. Another $206,214 went to develop games to promote nutrition. Uncle Sam cut a check for $60,000 to count trees in Henderson, Nevada.

More than $22 million went for the Agriculture, Forestry, and Fishing Program at the CDC, which duplicated similar efforts at the Department of Agriculture. The latter gave $181,966 for Tennessee to develop a smart phone app for special crop producers. NSF provided $300,000 to study the effectiveness of leaders of the European Parliament. A grant for $100,000 went to help the Massachusetts video game industry.

The Department of Defense spent $207 million on a duplicative second engine design for the F-35 fighter. NIH, also a repeat offender, spent $55,382 to study hookah smoking in Jordan. The Department of Homeland Security used $6,279 to purchase Snow Cone ice-making machines for emergency services in Michigan. The Agriculture Department, a perpetual waster, gave Oklahoma $93,000 to promote specialty crops. The ever busy NSF devoted $300,000 to developing a dance program to illustrate the origins of matter.

The National Institute for Aging paid researchers $610,908 to survey well-being around the world. The National Endowment for the Arts (NEA) provided $50,000 for a self-guided art tour in Wisconsin. The Technology Innovation Program spent $45 million subsidizing the research of numerous large, profit-making corporations. The Department of State spent $30,000 to send a New York City dance company to Indonesia. NSF—they never stop!—devoted a half million dollars to studying "information dissemination" on the Web.

The Department of Agriculture spent $12 million on a duplicative energy assistance program which both the Bush and Obama administrations proposed closing. U.S. AID consumed $156,273 celebrating its 50th anniversary of spending lots of money with little positive effect. The Agriculture Department—yet again!—devoted $15 million to repairing privately-owned rental property for low income people. The Rural Business Enterprise Grant program gave the Kriemhild Dairy Farms $55,660 to buy a new butter packing machine. NEA provided $50,000 to underwrite an international film festival in San Francisco.

The ever-busy NSF gave nearly a half million dollars for a children's chemistry theater. Some $50 million went for retrofitting diesel engines as part of an Environmental Protection Agency program which even the Obama administration wanted to kill. The Air Force Academy spent $51,474 to construct an outdoor worship center for "earth-based" religions. NSF provided $425,642 to study information dissemination and Indian politicians. A Missouri museum collected $300,000 for an exhibit on the history of transportation.

The National Endowment for Humanities paid $159,865 to send 16 university professors to Rome for five weeks. The duplicative Rail Line Relocation Program collected $10.5 million despite President Obama's attempt to end the outlay. The Department of State used $306,000 to bring European college students to America to learn civic activism. Columbia University collected $606,000 for a study of online dating. Uncle Sam gave $74,470 to a Utah museum to teach puppetry. The Appalachian Regional Commission, one of four "economic development" agencies, spent $68 million despite having no measurable effect on economic development.

NSF, ye gods!, used $198,195 to study what people expect from social media. Washington devoted $25,000 to transcribe a traditional love ballad in the Maldives. U.S. AID, another unrepentant recidivist, spent $15 million in a program permeated by waste and fraud to help Afghan war victims. NIH devoted $592,527 to study why chimpanzees throw objects. NSF used $130,987 to review the use of robots to promote language skills in preschoolers. The Transportation Department gave Louisiana $5.18 million to build the Steamboat Overlook Interpretive Center.

The never idle NSF gave $338,998 for researchers to, I am not making this up, study the impact of women on the Icelandic textile industry. The National Cowboy Poetry Gathering received $50,000 from Washington. The Agriculture Department devoted $742,907 to study using "targeted sheep grazing" against weeds. The Federal Highway Administration gave Washington, D.C. $83,000 to upgrade planter boxes in the median of a major street.

The Treasury Department spent $184 million to keep the paper dollar bill in circulation. NSF gave PBS $130,000 to redesign the website for one of its shows. Nearly half a million dollars went to the Christopher Columbus Fellowship Foundation, which no president has supported since its creation two decades ago, to promote activities "for the benefit of mankind."

The Transportation Security Administration overspent $184 million worth of taxpayer funds on airport security equipment it will never use.

The State Department built a consulate building in northern Afghanistan and THEN decided it was indefensible, wasting the $80 million that went into the construction.

The State Department spent $500 million since last October to staff a large Iraqi police training program in Iraq, a program that will likely be terminated by the end of the year with little discernible successes or improvements relative to Iraqi police forces.

The Navy almost completed the construction of two brand new Navy ships only to THEN decide they were no longer needed just before their construction was complete, expending another $10 billion to turn the unused and almost completed ships to scrap metal.

The General Services Administration wasted $832,000 on a Las Vegas party that was thinly disguised as a "conference."

Just these five examples above, of random, wasteful spending totals about $1.075 billion.

However, we can make a distinction that these random acts of disgraceful and wasteful spending are different from the "systemic wasteful spending" acts that occur every day of every year in the same basic manner: But what about the following?

Medicare and Medicaid lose about $110 to $150 billion annually to waste, inefficiencies, and criminal fraud.

Social Security loses about $125 billion annually to waste, inefficiencies and criminal fraud.

We have documented how just one of the Federal government's unemployment programs loses $19 billion annually to waste, inefficiencies, and criminal fraud.

The IRS admits it does not collect about $385 billion every year that is legally due to the Federal government but is not collected from tax evaders.

The National Science Foundation has an annual budget of about $6.9 billion but wastes most of that on idiotic projects (e.g. studying when dogs became man's best friend).

These systemic wasteful spending effort costs the American taxpayer about $665.9 billion a year. Since the beginning of the Obama administration three and a half years ago, this annual estimate comes out to about $2.331 TRILLION in total.

Thus, just these two types of wasteful spending examples over the past three and a half years come out to about $2.332 TRILLION. Keep this $2.332 TRILLION in the back of your mind, we will come back to it shortly.

Let's just take one simple example: Solar Energy, a key topic for Obama. The NOVA television report on how a California family had taken a typical suburban home and had it retrofitted with solar technology to make it near energy independent. The bottom line was that for about $60,000, a house could almost be taken off the grid and be made nearly energy independent.

Last year in the midst of the Solyndra debacle, it was widely reported that the Chinese had reduced their solar panel expense by about 30%. If we assume that the NOVA house solar energy retrofit cost of $60,000 consisted of $40,000 in equipment costs and $20,000 in installation costs, that house retrofit today would cost about $48,000 ($20,000 plus a 30% reduction in the $40,000 equipment cost).

Now let's take this new cost estimate and combine it with the $2.332 TRILLION in waste we identified above. If we divide the $2.332 TRILLION by the $48,000 unit cost of retrofit, if the political class and Federal government had been totally efficient, effective, and forward thinking, we could have used the $2.332 TRILLION to retrofit almost 49,000,000 U.S. homes with enough solar technology to make them almost totally energy independent.

If you look at U.S. Census data from 2009 you will see that there are about 73,000,000 million single family, detached home in the United States. This becomes the most damning piece of wasteful spending information that could ever be provided: if the government had funneled its wasted spending from just the past three and a half years into solar retrofits, about two thirds of every single family detached home in the COUNTRY would now be almost totally energy dependent.

What would that have meant for every American and our nation?

Household energy costs would be substantially reduced, freeing up household income to be used to grow the economy.

Untold number of jobs would have been created to install and service the new solar energy infrastructure.

If global warming actually exists, turning just about every single American family home into a solar energy generator would greatly have reduced our carbon footprint.

From a foreign policy perspective, we could care less about what happened in the Middle East since the need for their petroleum would have vanished.

There would no longer be a need for politicians like Obama to give away taxpayer wealth to non-viable alternative energy companies that also just happened to raise campaign cash for him and other politicians.

What about the $787 billion stimulus plan approved by Congress in February of 2012?.

Congressman Mark Schauer, who read and voted for the stimulus bill, told his constituents that there was no pork or earmarks in stimulus bill. Congressman Schauer pledged "vigorous oversight" to ensure the stimulus was "*administered efficiently and effectively*)

"Researchers at Penn State University received $1.57 million to search for fossils in Argentina"

"$100,000 for socially conscious puppet shows."

"The National Institutes of Health got $219,000 in funds to study whether female college students are more likely to "hook up" after drinking alcohol."

"A dinner cruise company based in Chicago received nearly $1 million in funds to combat terrorism."

$6 million to Hillary Clinton's pollster's Washington DC public relations firm to preserve three jobs.

"Two million dollars in stimulus money went to build a replica railroad as a tourist attraction in Carson City, Nev."

"Half a million dollars went to Arizona State University to study the genetic makeup of ants to determine distinctive roles in ant colonies"

"$450,000 went to the University of Arizona to study the division of labor in ant colonies."

"The State University of New York at Buffalo won $390,000 to study young adults who drink malt liquor and smoke marijuana."

"The University of Hawaii collected $210,000 to study the learning patterns of honeybees"

"$5 million grant from the Department of Energy to create a geothermal energy system for the Oak Ridge City Center shopping mall ... the mall has been losing tenants for years and is mostly empty."

"$4.7 million that Lockheed Martin received to conduct advance research of supersonic jet travel"

Unbelievable; how much better would we be if the political class had any kind of ability to lead, govern and set good priorities? Within four years, wasteful government spending could have been funneled into making the U.S. energy independent.

Let's give an example of some of the outlandish spending in the past decades. Some of those expenditures included spending from The National Endowment for the Humanities for a $25,000 grant in

13

1977 to study why people cheat, lie and act rudely on local Virginia tennis courts, the Office of Education for spent $219,592 in 1978 to develop a curriculum to teach college students how to watch television, and the Environmental Protection Agency spent an extra $1.2 million in 1980 to preserve a Trenton, New Jersey sewer as a historical monument.

Let's continue with more waste. The Obama administration has spent at least $3.469 billion on crony owned alternative energy companies that have all either gone bankrupt or are in the process of going bankrupt. If that $3.469 billion had been used to retrofit U.S. homes for solar independence, rather than be totally wasted on failing and failed companies, the entire city of Tallahassee, Florida would now be mostly off the grid and would be mostly energy independent. This accomplishment would dwarf all of the non-accomplishments of the failed companies Obama gave Federal dollars to.

Rather than focusing on efforts like those covered above to make taxpayer wealth useful in making the U.S. a better country, in this case energy independent, the political class focuses only on their own careers, self-interest, and personal enrichment. I never understood why they never address the issue of wasteful spending: is it because they do not know how to, they do not want to, and they do not care to, given the good that could come from cleaning up the waste and fraud.

Whatever their reason, we are living with their apathy, lack of leadership, and lack of positive results every day. No problems solved, massive amounts of wealth wasted. Term limits and dumping out all incumbent politicians at every election cannot come soon enough. We need people in D.C. that can do the simple math above, formulate plans, and then clean up the horrific mess the current set of politicians have left us with nothing to show in return for TRILLIONS of our tax dollars.

Please take note: the above examples of waste and how that could have been translated into energy independence efforts does not include the spending waste that is rampant in the bloated Civil Service Employment ranks, food stamp, Postal Service, TSA and other large Federal departments. Thus, the lost opportunity is actually far worse than the examples outlined above.

It's quite a list of silly and frivolous government expenditures. But it is only a small beginning in the recent few years. Even if we save all the money from killing these programs the America Government still would be going broke. Much more needs to be cut.

Advocates of federal programs believe that Washington is the best place to create and administer the programs. They believe that government can allocate resources much better than the private sector. The private sector points out that the inefficient use of tax dollars siphons money out of the general economy.

If our appointed officials won't get rid of ridiculous programs like these, they won't take on serious programs like Social Security, Medicare, Health Care and the overabundance of Civil Service Employees. And if they won't do that, then we might as well write off the secure future of our children.

We'll find out who will win this argument in November when you decide. But before you do decide, take a good look at the following chapters. They will reveal to you the true cost to our nation if we remain as sheep or status quo.

PART – 2

LACK OF FISCAL RESPONSIBILITY

Soaring government spending and trillion-dollar budget deficits have brought fiscal responsibility and reducing government waste back onto the national agenda. President Barack Obama identified 0.004 of 1 percent of the federal budget as wasteful and proposed eliminating this $140 million from his $3.6 trillion fiscal year 2010 budget request. Aiming higher, the president more recently proposed partially offsetting a costly new government health entitlement by reducing $622 billion in Medicare and Medicaid "waste and inefficiencies" over the next decade. Taxpayers may wonder why reducing such waste is now merely a bargaining chip for new spending rather than an end in itself.

It is possible to reduce spending and balance the budget. In the 1980s and 1990s, Washington consistently spent $21,000 per household (adjusted for inflation). Simply returning to that level would balance the budget by 2012 without any tax hikes.

Alternatively, merely returning to the 2008 (prerecession) spending level of $25,000 per household (adjusted for inflation) would likely balance the budget by 2019 without any tax hikes.

Not Easy, but Necessary

Reducing wasteful spending is not easy. Even the most useless programs are passionately supported by the armies of recipients, administrators, and lobbyists who benefit from their existence. Identifying inefficiencies and abuses is much easier than devising a system to fix them. Many lawmakers focus more on bringing home earmarks than on performing the less exciting task of government oversight. Exasperated taxpayers see the cost of government rise with no end in sight.

Of course, eliminating waste cannot balance the budget. Lawmakers must also rein in spending by reforming Social Security and Medicare and by eliminating government activities that are no longer affordable. Yet government waste is the low-hanging fruit that lawmakers must clean up in order to build credibility with the public for larger reforms.

Congress has allowed government employees to spend tax dollars on iPods, jewelry, gambling, exotic dance clubs, and $13,500 steak dinners. If lawmakers cannot even reduce this kind of waste, fraud, and abuse, taxpayers will be less likely to trust them to reform Social Security and Medicare.

Six Categories of Waste

The six categories of wasteful and unnecessary spending are:

18

Programs that should be devolved to state and local governments;

Programs that could be better performed by the private sector;

Mistargeted programs whose recipients should not be entitled to government benefits;

Outdated and unnecessary programs;

Duplicative programs; and

Inefficiency, mismanagement, and fraud.

The first four categories are generally subjective, and reasonable people can disagree on whether a given federal program falls under their purview. Yet the final two categories duplication and inefficiency, mismanagement, and fraud are comparatively easy to identify and oppose. Thus, they are heavily represented in the examples of government waste below:

The federal government made at least $72 billion in improper payments in 2008.

Washington spends $92 billion on corporate welfare (excluding TARP) versus $71 billion on homeland security.

Washington spends $25 billion annually maintaining unused or vacant federal properties.

Government auditors spent the past five years examining all federal programs and found that 22 percent of them costing taxpayers a total of $123 billion annually fail to show any positive impact on the populations they serve.

The Congressional Budget Office published a "Budget Options" series identifying more than $100 billion in potential spending cuts.

Examples from multiple Government Accountability Office (GAO) reports of wasteful duplication include 342 economic development programs; 130 programs serving the disabled; 130 programs serving at-risk youth; 90 early childhood development programs; 75 programs funding international education, cultural, and training exchange activities; and 72 safe water programs.

Washington will spend $2.6 million training Chinese prostitutes to drink more responsibly on the job.

A GAO audit classified nearly half of all purchases on government credit cards as improper, fraudulent, or embezzled. Examples of taxpayer-funded purchases include gambling, mortgage payments, liquor, lingerie, iPods, Xboxes, jewelry, Internet dating services, and Hawaiian vacations. In one extraordinary example, the Postal Service spent $13,500 on one dinner at a Ruth's Chris Steakhouse, including "over 200 appetizers and over $3,000 of alcohol, including more than 40 bottles of wine costing more than $50 each and brand-name liquor such as Courvoisier, Belvedere and Johnny Walker Gold." The eighty-one guests consumed an average of $167 worth of food and drink apiece.

Federal agencies are delinquent on nearly 20 percent of employee travel charge cards, costing taxpayers hundreds of millions of dollars annually.

The Securities and Exchange Commission spent $3.9 million rearranging desks and offices at its Washington, DC, headquarters.

The Pentagon recently spent $998,798 shipping two nineteen-cent washers from South Carolina to Texas and $293,451 sending an eighty-nine-cent washer from South Carolina to Florida.

Over half of all farm subsidies go to commercial farms, which report average household incomes of $200,000.

Health care fraud is estimated to cost taxpayers more than $60 billion annually.

A GAO audit found that ninety-five Pentagon weapons systems suffered from a combined $295 billion in cost overruns.

The refusal of many federal employees to fly coach costs taxpayers $146 million annually in flight upgrades.

Washington will spend $126 million in 2009 to enhance the Kennedy family legacy in Massachusetts. Additionally, Senator John Kerry (D-MA) diverted $20 million from the 2010 defense budget to subsidize a new Edward M. Kennedy Institute.

Federal investigators have launched more than twenty criminal fraud investigations related to the TARP financial bailout.

Despite trillion-dollar deficits, a $200,000 request by California Rep. Howard Berman: for the Providence Holy Cross Foundation tattoo removal violence prevention program in Mission Hills in 2009.

In California in 2011; $190,000 for the Buffalo Bill Historical Center in Cody, Wyoming; and $75,000 for the Totally Teen Zone in Albany, Georgia.

The federal government owns more than fifty thousand vacant homes.

The Federal Communications Commission spent $350,000 to sponsor NASCAR driver David Gilliland.

Members of Congress have spent hundreds of thousands of taxpayer dollars supplying their offices with popcorn machines, plasma televisions, DVD equipment, ionic air fresheners, camcorders, and signature machines plus $24,730 leasing a Lexus, $1,434 on a digital camera, and $84,000 on personalized calendars.

More than $13 billion in Iraq aid has been classified as wasted or stolen. Another $7.8 billion cannot be accounted for.

Fraud related to Hurricane Katrina spending is estimated to top $2 billion. In addition, debit cards provided to hurricane victims were used to pay for Caribbean vacations, NFL tickets, Dom Perignon champagne, "Girls Gone Wild" videos, and at least one sex change operation.

Auditors discovered that 900,000 of the 2.5 million recipients of emergency Katrina assistance provided false names, addresses, or Social Security numbers or submitted multiple applications.

Congress gave Alaska Airlines $500,000 to paint a Chinook salmon on a Boeing 737.

The Transportation Department will subsidize up to $2,000 per flight for direct flights between Washington, DC, and the small hometown of Congressman Hal Rogers (R-KY) but only on Monday mornings and Friday evenings, when lawmakers, staff, and lobbyists usually fly. Rogers is a member of the Appropriations Committee, which writes the Transportation Department's budget.

Washington has spent $3 billion re-sanding beaches even as this new sand washes back into the ocean.

A Department of Agriculture report concedes that much of the $2.5 billion in "stimulus" funding for broadband Internet will be wasted.

The Defense Department wasted $100 million on unused flight tickets and never bothered to collect refunds even though the tickets were refundable.

Washington spends $60,000 per hour shooting Air Force One photo-ops in front of national landmarks.

Over one recent eighteen-month period, air force and navy personnel used government-funded credit cards to charge at least $102,400 on admission to entertainment events, $48,250 on gambling, $69,300 on cruises, and $73,950 on exotic dance clubs and prostitutes.

Members of Congress are set to pay themselves $90 million to increase their franked mailings for the 2010 election year.

Congress has ignored efficiency recommendations from the Department of Health and Human Services that would save $9 billion annually.

Taxpayers are funding paintings of high-ranking government officials at a cost of up to $50,000 apiece.

The state of Washington sent one-dollar food stamp checks to 250,000 households in order to raise state caseload figures and trigger $43 million in additional federal funds.

Suburban families are receiving large farm subsidies for the grass in their backyards. Subsidies that many of these families never requested and do not want.

Congress appropriated $20 million for "commemoration of success" celebrations related to Iraq and Afghanistan.

Homeland Security employee purchases include sixty-three-inch plasma TVs, iPods, and $230 for a beer brewing kit.

Two drafting errors in the 2005 Deficit Reduction Act resulted in a $2 billion taxpayer cost.

North Ridgeville, Ohio, received $800,000 in "stimulus" funds for a project that its mayor described as "a long way from the top priority."

The National Institutes of Health spends $1.3 million per month to rent a lab that it cannot use.

Congress spent $2.4 billion on ten new jets that the Pentagon insists it does not need and will not use.

Lawmakers diverted $13 million from Hurricane Katrina relief spending to build a museum celebrating the Army Corps of Engineers the agency partially responsible for the failed levees that flooded New Orleans.

Medicare officials mailed $50 million in erroneous refunds to 230,000 Medicare recipients.

Audits showed $34 billion worth of Department of Homeland Security contracts contained significant waste, fraud, and abuse.

Washington spent $1.8 million to help build a private golf course in Atlanta, Georgia.

The Advanced Technology Program spends $150 million annually subsidizing private businesses; 40 percent of this funding goes to Fortune 500 companies.

Congressional investigators were able to receive $55,000 in federal student loan funding for a fictional college they created to test the Department of Education.

The Conservation Reserve program pays farmers $2 billion annually not to farm their land.

The Commerce Department has lost 1,137 computers since 2001, many containing Americans' personal data.

Pick the Low-Hanging Fruit

Because many of these examples of waste overlap, it is not possible to determine their exact total cost. Yet it is evident that Washington loses hundreds of billions of dollars annually on spending that most Americans would certainly consider wasteful. Lawmakers seeking to rein in spending and budget deficits should begin by eliminating this least justifiable spending while also addressing long-term entitlement costs.

PART - 3

JUST PLAIN HEINOUS

A report prepared by Senator Tom Coburn's (R-OK) office reveals taxpayers shelled out $615,000 so the University of California at Santa Cruz could digitize Grateful Dead photographs, tickets, backstage passes, fliers, shirts, and other memorabilia.

"This is one of the first efforts to preserve and share cultural and historical artifacts of the baby boom generation, a group that includes seventy-six million Americans," representatives of the Institute of Museum and Library Services explained.

So let the baby boomers pay for it out of their own pockets.

When taxpayers aren't shelling out money for music memorabilia, they're busy paying for the other projects listed in Coburn's report. Here are a few named in the report:

They supply $175 million a year so the Department of Veterans Affairs can maintain buildings it doesn't use, including a pink octagonal monkey house in Dayton, Ohio.

They pinch pennies so a federal grant program can distribute $1 million to zoos to post bits of poetry to plaques on zoo premises.

They cushion the federal coffers so the Monkton, Vermont, Conservation Commission can build a "critter crossing" for $150,000.

They file honest tax returns so the Internal Revenue Service can deliver $112 million in undeserved tax refunds to prisoners who filed fraudulent returns.

They fork over their hard-earned dollars so Denali National Park in Alaska can afford nearly $1.5 million worth of new toilets.

As Coburn puts it, examples like these are too numerous to count.

"Worse yet," he writes, "they are costing us billions even as we borrow huge sums just to keep the government operating at a basic level."

The Wastebook reveals the madness—but it can't stop it. Fortunately, Coburn says, the examples it cites could easily be eliminated.

As the curtain closed on 2011, Coburn and his staff decided to take a closer look at the federal government's ledger. He found $6.9 billion dollars in what the senator called "egregious" waste. Though this total was just a fraction of the $3.599 trillion spent in 2011, some of the examples were just plain heinous.

Take for instance the $35.38 million given to political parties to help pay for the national conventions leading up to the presidential election. You may think this money is restricted to security for elected officials, but instead, the taxpayer money "could help pay for the stages, confetti, balloons, food, and booze" for attendees.

Among many other examples, lets shed light on $30 million sent to Pakistan for agriculture assistance before the program was deemed ineffective and canceled; $6 million for small airports, 62.5 percent of which never met a single grant objective; $4.38 billion in wartime contracting waste and fraud; another $14.3 million (for a grand total of $65 million) for Alaska's famous bridge to nowhere; $120 million in benefits to dead federal employees; $17.8 million in foreign aid to China., the largest holder of our federal debt.

At some point it's easy to lose sight of what these numbers mean, but some anecdotes serve as a reminder that when one constituency wins, another loses. Los Angeles allegedly "redirected $1 million in taxpayer money intended to help the city's homeless and low income residents to a wealthy international architecture firm designing a NFL football stadium."

Furthermore, as much as $1 billion in taxpayer money intended as a tax credit for energy efficient home improvements was given to those who have no record of owning a home, including prisoners and children. And while it may be illegal for humans to do cocaine, taxpayers funded a study looking for connections between cocaine usage and sexual habits...in quails. The report outlined far too many examples to list here. And some sound so unbelievable; I recommend you just take a look for yourself.

Can we depend on the government to take care of its money?

That's a tough call because government bureaucrats never take care of your money as carefully as you would take care of it yourself. More important, bureaucrats spend money on what government wants, not what you want—which is the whole point of taxing away your money.

Without authorization, for instance, the feds spent $19.6 million annually on the International Fund for Ireland. Sounds like a noble cause, but the money went for projects like pony-trekking centers and golf videos.

Congressional budget-cutters spared the $440,000 spent annually to have attendants' push buttons on the fully automated Capitol Hill elevators used by representatives and senators.

Last year, the National Endowment for the Humanities spent $4.2 million to conduct a nebulous "National Conversation on Pluralism and Identity." Obviously, talk radio wasn't considered good enough.

The Pentagon and Central Intelligence Agency channeled some $11 million to psychics who might provide special insights about various foreign threats. This was the disappointing "Stargate" program.

The Department of Education spent $34 million supposedly helping Americans become better shoppers and homemakers. Wasn't it about time?

The federal government has also proposed spending $14 million for a new army museum, although there already were forty-seven army museums around the country.

Dubious government spending schemes abound since bureaucrats play with other people's money. For example, the National Institutes of Mental Health (NIMH) spent $70,029 to see if the degu, a diurnal South American rodent, can help us better understand jet lag...NIMH spent $77,826 to study "Coping with Change in Czechoslovakia"...$100,271 to see if volunteering is good for older people...$124,910 to reduce "School Phobia" in children...$161,913 to study "Israeli reactions to SCUD Attacks during the Gulf War"...and $187,042 to study the quality of life in Hawaii.

Over the years, political wrangling twists the most noble-sounding government programs beyond recognition. Take, for example, the Social Security Administration's $25-billion-a-year Supplemental Security Income (SSI) program. Almost 250,000 children qualify for SSI checks because they can't participate in "age-appropriate activities." Worse, thousands of prisoners get SSI checks relating to their alleged disabilities—costing taxpayers about $20 million a year.

That's not all. In Denver, the government reportedly sent $160,000 to recipients at their "official address"—a tavern. A San Francisco addict used his SSI check to buy drugs, which he subsequently sold on the street for a profit. A Van Nuys, California, alcoholic received a $26,000 SSI check, then spent the money on a van and two cars, which he subsequently wrecked while driving drunk. Los Angeles SSI recipients reportedly faked mental illness and had a doctor concoct false medical records so they could pocket $45,000 worth of checks. An estimated seventy-nine thousand alcoholics and drug addicts are believed to spend SSI checks—some $360 million annually—on their habits.

Again and again, programs aimed at the poor are captured by well-heeled interest groups. For example, the Commerce Department's US Travel and Tourism Administration (USTTA) gave away $440,000 in so-called "disaster relief" to western ski resort operators when there wasn't much snow.

The Economic Development Administration spent "anti-poverty" funds to help build a $1.2 million football stadium in spiffy Spartanburg, South Carolina. During the summer, it will serve as a practice facility for the National Football League Carolina Panthers, and the rest of the year it will be used by Wofford College, which has a $50 million endowment.

Look at one of the most enduring legacies of Lyndon Johnson's "War on Poverty": the Appalachian Regional Commission. It was billed as help for an impoverished region. During the past three decades, this bureaucracy you've probably never heard of has spent $6.2 billion, yet the region remains impoverished.

Where did the money go? Two-thirds was spent building twenty-six highways connecting well-to-do urban centers. The money went to construction workers whose wages are definitely above average. Despite revolutionary talk in Washington, the Appalachian Regional Commission goes on and on.

Or take the plight of the family farmer. I know you've been regaled about wasteful spending on agricultural subsidies, so I'll just cite a single intriguing example: 1.6 million farm subsidy checks for $1.3

billion, mailed to urban ZIP codes during the past decade. New York City "farmers" pocketed $7 million during the past decade, Washington, DC, "farmers" $10 million, Los Angeles "farmers" $10.7 million, Minneapolis "farmers" $48 million, Miami "farmers" $54.5 million, and Phoenix "farmers" $71.5 million. Among those on the take, to the tune of $1.3 million: forty-seven "farmers" in Beverly Hills, California—one of America's wealthiest cities.

A lot of government spending is justified as necessary for national security. For instance, maritime subsidies supposedly help maintain a fleet for an emergency. Laws require government agencies to use US-flag vessels that are US-built, US-owned, and US-crewed, costing two to four times the world market price of comparable vessels available elsewhere. When the US Department of Agriculture and Agency for International Development give away surplus grain, they must use US-flag vessels for at least 75 percent of shipments, adding $233 million to the taxpayer burden. The US-flag requirement adds $1.75 billion to the defense budget. Subsidy per maritime job: over $100,000.

The defense budget is larded with waste not because it's run by bad guys but because it's big and bureaucrats are, as always, spending other people's money. The Pentagon has an "operational support airlift" consisting of some 500 airplanes and 100 helicopters for flying military brass and civilian bureaucrats on 1,800 trips a month—costing taxpayers $380 million a year. Many of the destinations are served by commercial airlines.

In 1995, the Pentagon announced it would spend $5.1 million to build a new eighteen-hole golf course at Andrews Air Force Base in suburban Maryland, which already has two. *Golf Digest* reported there are nineteen military golf courses around Washington, DC.

Why a new golf course? One Pentagon official was quoted as saying "a lot of golf gets played out there. On Saturday mornings, people are standing on top of each other."

Can It Continue?

How can such outrageous waste go on year after year? Simple: Bureaucrats aren't doling out their money, so they have little incentive to be responsible. Politically connected special interests, which are usually better off than the average taxpayer, seem to get most of the loot.

The most powerful special interest is government itself. In fiscal year 1993, the federal government owned 569,556 vehicles—one for every six full-time employees. Included were 117 limousines. The government's fleet has expanded by more than 130,000 vehicles since the Grace Commission called for it to be cut in half more than a decade ago.

Government officials multiply the number of regulations regardless of the waste they cause. For example, the Defense Department has 1,357 pages of regulations about how officials travel. Complying with these regulations adds about 30 percent to travel costs. If the Pentagon adopted the best practices of private companies, it could save an estimated $650 million to $840 million every year. Of course, government regulations cause enormous waste in the private sector—tax compliance costs alone run into the billions—but that's a vast subject unto itself.

The federal government wastes money through grants to the most politically powerful environmental lobbyists. For example, between 1990 and 1994, the Natural Resources Defense Council got $246,622; Defenders of Wildlife, $1,285,658; Environmental Defense Fund, $1,493,976; and the World Wildlife Fund, $26,584,335. Altogether, environmental lobbyists collected $156,644,352 during this period. Every one pushes the federal government to enact more regulations.

Whenever you hear a politician propose that government take over some private business, like New York's troubled Long Island Lighting Company, there should be red flags all over the place, because government operation means high costs. At the US Government Printing Office, for instance, costs are estimated to be 50 percent higher than in the private printing industry. If the US air traffic control system were transferred to private companies and the services paid by user fees, taxpayer savings would probably be around $18 billion over the next five years.

With a $1.5 trillion annual budget, the feds take so much of your money that they can't possibly keep track of it even if they wanted to. For example, a contractor sold $27 electronic relays to the government's Strategic Petroleum Reserve for between $484 and $521 apiece. The Department of Energy paid some of its employees $5,000 a year to lose weight—the outlays totaled $10 million a year. The owner of a California apartment building got Department of Housing and Urban Development subsidies, and then illicitly diverted $610,000 into his own accounts. One "farmer" collected $1.6 million in government insurance payments for nonexistent crops. Forty-three people in New York City pocketed over $40 million in phony food stamp claims. Five Floridians stole $20 million from Medicare—part of the estimated $17 billion of annual Medicare fraud.

What to do about such waste? The government is crawling with auditors, and there have been a zillion investigations, yet waste goes on. Citizens Against Government Waste will continue to be a watchdog. The only long-term solution, though, is to somehow cut big government down to size. Only when it's much smaller will you be able to keep more of your hard-earned money, which, after all, is yours.

PART – 4

OUTRAGEOUS EXAMPLES OF YOUR MONEY BEING WASTED

Government spending must be cut. The national debt exceeds the annual GDP. Total unfunded liabilities are fourteen times as much, more than $200 trillion. Once again, government spending must be cut.

Unfortunately, the biggest pots of money have the largest number of dedicated guardians. Interest on the national debt must be paid, unless Uncle Sam is prepared to default, like Greece. Seniors form a phalanx around Social Security and Medicare. Medicaid already ill serves the poor and underpays doctors. The military-industrial complex fights as hard for weapons spending today as it did against communism during the Cold War.

About all that's left is domestic discretionary spending, roughly 15 percent of the budget. Most everyone in Washington talks about freezing or cutting these outlays, but nothing ever happens. Politicians want pork to distribute, and interest groups want grants, loans, loan guarantees, tax preferences, and all manner of other privileges funded by government. Whether Republicans or Democrats are in control, the taxpayers' money continues to be wasted.

The U.S budget deficit for fiscal year 2011 is $1.3 trillion, the second largest shortfall in history.

The nation only ran a larger deficit for the 2009 fiscal year, which included the dramatic collapse of financial markets and a huge bailout effort by the government. The nation's deficit that year was $1.412 trillion.

This year's deficit is slightly higher than fiscal year 2010, when the nation ran a $1.293 trillion deficit. Fiscal years run through Sept. 30.

With the US budget deficit at $1.3 trillion and the National Debt in August 2012 just under 16 Trillion Dollars. That means every "discretionary" outlay effectively came from borrowed money and loans that must be repaid by taxpayers in a weak economy made permanently smaller by the diversion of otherwise productive resources to political projects.

If Congress doesn't have the courage to cut even these expenditures, then what hope is there that it will bring the nation back from hundreds of trillions in future overspending?

Senator Coburn is a rarity on Capitol Hill, a scourge of the wasteful foolishness that emanates from the Potomac. In his view "perhaps there was no bigger waste of the taxpayers' money in 2011 than Congress itself." Lots of people talk about "waste," but few do anything about it. Coburn identified one hundred really dumb projects and collected them in the "2011 Wastebook: A Guide to Some of the Most Wasteful and Low Priority Government Spending of 2011." It is a great place to start cutting unnecessary government.

Number one is obvious with the approach of another presidential election. As of November 2011, the Presidential Election Campaign Fund contained $35.38 million. What could be dumber than forcing the American people to pay for the campaigns and conventions of the very politicians who created today's mess? At least President Obama is helping to destroy the system by eschewing public funding.

The ninety-nine other examples of waste? The US Agency for International Development (US AID) spent $30 million to spur mango production and sales in Pakistan—and failed utterly. The air force spent $14 million to switch three radar stations to wind power; poor planning forced cancellation of one turbine and consideration of the same for the other two. The Federal Aviation Administration devoted $6 million to subsidize air service at small, underused airports.

A federal grant for $765,828 went to—I am not making this up, to quote Dave Barry—bring an International House of Pancakes franchise to Washington, DC. Although the famed "Bridge to Nowhere" might never be built, Uncle Sam still shelled out $15.3 million in project costs, including a fourteen-minute promotional video, on top of $50 million already absorbed by the Knik Arm Bridge. The Office of Personnel Management sent $120 million to dead federal employees (actually, they probably did less harm than the live ones!).

The Department of Transportation spent $529,689 to create the fourth visitor center around the fifty-four-mile Talimena Scenic Drive between Oklahoma and Arkansas. A check for $113,277 was cut to help the International Center for the History of Electronic Games to preserve "historic" video games. Washington helpfully gave almost $18 million in foreign aid to China—money effectively borrowed from China. The Department for Housing and Urban Development (HUD) provided a $484,000 grant to build a "Mellow Mushroom Pizza Bakers" restaurant in Texas.

Uncle Sam sent $100,000 to the Washington State Fruit Commission to stage a "celebrity chef fruit promotion road show" in Indonesia. US AID gave $10 million to an arts organization in Pakistan—a country threatened with disintegration—to produce local episodes of *Sesame Street*. Then there was $150,000 for the American Museum of Magic in Marshall, Michigan. Another HUD grant, this one for $1 million, went to a foreign architectural firm to move its headquarters from Santa Monica to Los Angeles. The federal government cut a check for $550,000 to underwrite a documentary on the impact of rock 'n' roll on the collapse of communism.

The National Institutes of Health (NIH) provided a $702,558 grant for the study of the impact of televisions and gas generators on villages in Vietnam. Hawaii's annual Chocolate Festival collected $48,700 from Washington. People who didn't own homes, such as children and prisoners, claimed as much as a billion dollars in tax credits for promoting energy efficiency in their houses. The Department of Commerce gave $936,818 to create a web TV soap opera on single moms to spur adoption of broadband.

Michigan received $75,000 to promote Christmas trees and poinsettias. The State Department spent $350,000 to underwrite an arts festival in Venice, Italy. NIH gave the University of Kentucky $175,587 to study the impact of cocaine on the sex drive of Japanese quail. A grant for $2 million went to Washington State's Walter Clore Wine and Culinary Center.

The Department of Agriculture spent $200 million—still not real money in the nation's capital—to promote industry groups, cooperatives, and corporations. The Centers for Disease Control and Prevention (CDC) spent $385,005 to survey what bus riders thought of HIV videos. Maine collected $95,000 to purchase iPads for kindergartners. The Agency for Health Research and Quality spent more than $1 million to get people to visit its website. The National Science Foundation (NSF) used $200,000 to see what the public thinks of politicians and climate change.

The Federal Highway Administration (FHA) gave $916,567 to underwrite horse-drawn carriage exhibits and survey shipwrecks in Wisconsin. The Veterans Administration spent $221,540 on a conference on disability ratings. NSF spent $300,000 for tourism podcasts in Alaska. The IRS used $862,000 to store unused furniture and equipment. NSF (again!) spent nearly a half million dollars to study whether people trust tweets from Twitter. US AID devoted $12 million to help the hapless Pakistanis use less energy.

The Oregon Cheese Guild received $50,400 to promote cheese. HUD gave $168 million, still pocket change in Washington, to the federally chartered Neighborhood Reinvestment Corporation, deemed unnecessary and duplicative by the Congressional Budget Office. The Agriculture Department, another multiple offender, spent $73,824 to encourage bed-and-breakfasts to use local produce. New Hampshire's Museum on the History of Skiing received $86,000.

Fraud and waste in wartime contracting may have cost about $4.4 billion. Now that's real money!

Uncle Sam spent $111,000 to send brewery experts to conduct classes in China. A grant for $24,632 went for the Milwaukee Public Museum to produce a 3-D virtual mummy unwrapping. NSF (won't it ever stop?) provided $149,990 for production of a guppy-to-fish video game. The Department of Agriculture spent $9.49 million on a duplicative program in management of foreign forests that even the White House wants to eliminate. Washington used $697,006 to beautify Las Vegas highways.

The ubiquitous NSF spent $764,825 to study student social networking. The equally wastrel Agriculture Department devoted $171,050 for a farm marketing effort in Vermont. The federal government paid $136,555 so teachers could retrace the steps of Chaucer's *Canterbury Tales*. The Energy Department's $231 million weatherization program was inefficient, wasteful, and duplicative.

US AID underwrote a $1.35 million "entrepreneurship initiative" in Barbados. The Coast Guard spent $24,450 on a float in the Mardi Gras. NSF (yet again!) spent $126,242 on a study of campaign websites. Salt Lake City received $150,000 to renovate a carriage house. The Department of Transportation spent $8.3 million to preserve covered bridges. Wine promotion benefited from $62,000 in federal promotional funds. Another $206,214 went to develop games to promote nutrition. Uncle Sam cut a check for $60,000 to count trees in Henderson, Nevada.

More than $22 million went for the Agriculture, Forestry, and Fishing Program at the CDC, which duplicated similar efforts at the Department of Agriculture. The latter gave $181,966 for

Tennessee to develop a smart phone app for special crop producers. NSF provided $300,000 to study the effectiveness of leaders of the European Parliament. A grant for $100,000 went to help the Massachusetts video game industry.

The Department of Defense spent $207 million on a duplicative second engine design for the F-35 fighter. NIH, also a repeat offender, spent $55,382 to study hookah smoking in Jordan. The Department of Homeland Security used $6,279 to purchase snow cone ice-making machines for emergency services in Michigan. The Agriculture Department, a perpetual waster, gave Oklahoma $93,000 to promote specialty crops. The ever busy NSF devoted $300,000 to developing a dance program to illustrate the origins of matter.

The National Institute for Aging paid researchers $610,908 to survey well-being around the world. The National Endowment for the Arts (NEA) provided $50,000 for a self-guided art tour in Wisconsin. The Technology Innovation Program spent $45 million subsidizing the research of numerous large, profit-making corporations. The Department of State spent $30,000 to send a New York City dance company to Indonesia. NSF—it never stops!—devoted a half million dollars to studying "information dissemination" on the web.

The Department of Agriculture spent $12 million on a duplicative energy assistance program that both the Bush and Obama administrations proposed closing. US AID consumed $156,273 celebrating its fiftieth anniversary of spending lots of money with little positive effect. The Agriculture Department—yet again!—devoted $15 million to repairing privately owned rental property for low-income people. The Rural Business Enterprise Grant program gave the Kriemhild Dairy Farms $55,660 to buy a new butter packing machine. NEA provided $50,000 to underwrite an international film festival in San Francisco.

The ever-busy NSF gave nearly a half million dollars for a children's chemistry theater. Some $50 million went for retrofitting diesel engines as part of an Environmental Protection Agency program that even the Obama administration wanted to kill. The Air Force Academy spent $51,474 to construct an outdoor worship center for "earth-based" religions. NSF provided $425,642 to study information dissemination and Indian politicians. A Missouri museum collected $300,000 for an exhibit on the history of transportation.

The National Endowment for Humanities paid $159,865 to send sixteen university professors to Rome for five weeks. The duplicative Rail Line Relocation Program collected $10.5 million despite President Obama's attempt to end the outlay. The Department of State used $306,000 to bring European college students to America to learn civic activism. Columbia University collected $606,000 for a study of online dating. Uncle Sam gave $74,470 to a Utah museum to teach puppetry. The Appalachian Regional Commission, one of four "economic development" agencies, spent $68 million despite having no measurable effect on economic development.

NSF ye gods! used $198,195 to study what people expect from social media. Washington devoted $25,000 to transcribe a traditional love ballad in the Maldives. US AID, another unrepentant recidivist, spent $15 million in a program permeated by waste and fraud to help Afghan war victims. NIH devoted $592,527 to study why chimpanzees throw objects. NSF used $130,987 to review the use of robots to promote language skills in preschoolers.

The Transportation Department gave Louisiana $5.18 million to build the Steamboat Overlook Interpretive Center.

The never idle NSF gave $338,998 for researchers to I am not making this up study the impact of women on the Icelandic textile industry. The National Cowboy Poetry Gathering received $50,000 from Washington. The Agriculture Department devoted $742,907 to study using "targeted sheep grazing" against weeds. The Federal Highway Administration gave Washington, DC, $83,000 to upgrade planter boxes in the median of a major street.

The Treasury Department spent $184 million to keep the paper dollar bill in circulation. NSF gave PBS $130,000 to redesign the website for one of its shows. Nearly half a million dollars went to the Christopher Columbus Fellowship Foundation, which no president has supported since its creation two decades ago, to promote activities "for the benefit of mankind."

It's quite a list of silly and frivolous government expenditures. But it is only a small beginning.

Save all the money from killing these programs and America still would be going broke. Much more needs to be cut.

However, Senator Coburn has provided a good starting point. Legislators of both parties insist that outlays must be reduced. Here is their chance.

If they won't get rid of ridiculous programs like these, they won't take on serious programs like Social Security and the Pentagon. And if they won't do that, then Uncle Sam might as well start filling out his papers to declare bankruptcy.

PART – 5

MILITARY WASTE AND FRAUD WITHIN OUR PENTAGON:

When it comes to wasting money, the Pentagon has no peer. In October 2011, Sen. Bernie Sanders (I-Vt.) highlighted what he called a "shocking" internal Pentagon report that concluded defense companies defrauded the military by $1.1 trillion.

"The ugly truth is that virtually all of the major defense contractors in this country for years have been engaged in systemic fraudulent behavior, while receiving hundreds of billions of dollars of taxpayer money," Sanders said in a statement. "With the country running a nearly $15 trillion national debt, my goal is to provide as much transparency as possible about what is happening with taxpayer money."

I is shocking to learn that the Pentagon wasted over $30 billion on private no-bid contracts for projects in Iraq and Afghanistan that will never come to fruition. However, considering the economic calamity currently defining the United States and its leadership, we should not be surprised. In an independent inquiry due to be submitted to Congress, the Commission on Wartime Contracting warns of waste and fraud in the Pentagon's contracting activities.

"Tens of billions of taxpayer dollars have been wasted through poor planning, vague and shifting requirements, inadequate competition, substandard contract management and oversight, lax accountability, weak interagency coordination, and subpar performance or outright misconduct by some contractors and federal employees," the co-chairs of the panel, Christopher Shays and Michael Thibault, wrote in a commentary in the *Washington Post*.

Examples cited by the Commission include a $300 million power plant in Kabul. It is feared that the Afghan government will not have the technical means by which to run the plant on its own, nor the funds to sustain its operation. Other examples of wasteful contracts include a $40 million prison in Iraq that the government there "did not want and that was never finished," according to Shays and Thibault.

One of the major downfalls in the Pentagon's contracting process is believed by the Commission to be the lack of competition in the no-bid process. In fact, no-bid contracts nearly tripled from $50 billion in 2001 to $140 billion in 2010 following the attacks of September 11, 2011. The Pentagon defends non-competitive no-bid contracts claiming that there is often only one supplier of certain goods and that wartime efforts offer an unusual and compelling urgency. "There have been many instances because of wartime needs where a long, lengthy competitive bid contract process does not serve the needs of the warfighters," says Pentagon spokesman Colonel Dave Lapan.

Government Accountability Office (GAO) found that the Defense Logistics Agency had no use for parts worth $7.1 billion, more than half of the $13.7 billion in equipment stacked in Defense Department warehouses.

The investigation was requested by Sen. Bernie Sanders (I-Vt.), a Senate Budget Committee member who has closely monitored Pentagon waste and fraud. "The waste of taxpayer dollars is unbelievable," Sanders said. "At a time when the country has a $13 trillion national debt and is struggling with huge unmet needs, it is outrageous that the Defense Department continues to waste huge sums of money for spare parts that the military doesn't need."

The Pentagon has long been accustomed to more spending and fewer questions than other agencies. Pentagon spending has been on a steep rise almost without interruption since President Reagan took office in 1981. The Pentagon is not audited. Its books are not in a condition that even permits an audit; its comptroller currently estimates that an audit might be possible—beginning in 2017.

The Pentagon spends well over half a trillion dollars a year, not counting war spending. It has a proven record of losing and wasting funds, spending funds that were not authorized by Congress, and tolerating a level of fraud that Congress would not stand for in other federal departments. Here's how it happens:

The Department of Defense has 98 major weapons systems in its "portfolio." According to the Government Accountability Office, in the last two years alone the cost of those weapons has grown by $135 billion beyond initial estimates. For example, Congress authorized the Joint Strike Fighter, intended as a replacement for all the jets used by the Air Force, Navy and Marines, as a $284 billion program. It is now expected to cost $318 billion. That $34 billion difference would almost pay for the entire Pell grant (college financial aid) program.

But all of this excessive waste of our tax dollars did not just start during this administration. It has been a long standing practice in the DOD. I am not advocating gutting the defense budget. What I am highlighting is the absolute need to establish stronger project controls on expenditures, contract awards, project over runs and the elimination of pet projects that benefit the political constituents.

Let's look at the past decade to see just how long this outrageous spending has been going on and with the full knowledge of Congress and the White House.

For one thing, there's the single question of scale. For fiscal year 1996, the Pentagon budget was $265 billion ($7 billion more than it requested). That's 5 percent of our gross national product, a larger percentage than in virtually any other industrialized nation. In absolute dollars (not as a percentage of GNP), the Pentagon shells out 3½ times more than the next largest military spender (Russia), 6½ times more than Britain, 7½ times more than France, 7¼ times more than Japan, and 8½ times more than Germany.

The Stockholm International Peace Research Institute has a new report out highlighting global military expenditures. As the above chart indicates, the U.S. retains a healthy lead.

Our military budget is bigger than the next nine largest military budgets combined, and sixteen times larger than the combined military budgets of all of our "regional adversaries" Cuba, Syria, Iran, Iraq, North Korea, and Libya. It accounts percent of all military spending on the planet (in comparison, our economy is only 22 percent of the world total). As enormous as the Pentagon's budget is, there's more military spending buried elsewhere—in the Department of Energy's production of fuel for nuclear weapons, in the military portion of the NASA budget, in the Veterans Administration, etc. By adding in these hidden military expenses, the Center for Defense Information (CDI), a Washington think tank run by retired generals and admirals, concluded that we spend a total of over $600 billion a year on the military. And it is expected to top &700 billion in the next decade.

But that doesn't include what we have to pay for past Pentagon budgets. The CDI went back to 1941 and multiplied the military's percentage of each year's budget by the deficit for that year. Using that method, it figured that interest on past military spending cost us $167 billion in fiscal 1996. The War Resisters League went all the way back to 1789 and came up with $291 billion. Since the CDI's estimates are lower, let's be conservative and use them. Adding them together gives us a figure for total military spending past and present of $494 billion a year ($9.5 billion a week, $1.3 billion a day).

Waste beyond your wildest dreams. But just the scale of the Pentagon's budget alone can't explain its prodigious ability to waste money. Another quality is required: world-class incompetence. There are so many examples of this that they tend to blur together, numbing the mind. Here are just a few: According to a

US Senate hearing, $13 billion the Pentagon handed out to weapons contractors between 1985 and 1995 was simply "lost." Another $15 billion remains unaccounted for because of "financial management troubles." That's $28 billion—right off the top—that has simply disappeared....

According to the Bulletin of the Atomic Scientists, every single one of the top ten weapons contractors was convicted of or admitted to defrauding the government between 1980 and 1992. For example:

* Grumman paid the government $20 million to escape criminal liability for coercing subcontractors into making political contributions.

* Lockheed was convicted of paying millions in bribes to obtain classified planning documents.

* Northrop was fined $17 million for falsifying test data on its cruise missiles and fighter jets.

* Rockwell was fined $5.5 million for committing criminal fraud against the air force.

In another study, the Project on Government Oversight (PGO) searched public records from October 1989 to February 1994 and found in just that 4½-year period eighty-five instances of fraud, waste, and abuse in weapons contracting. For example:

Boeing, Grumman, Hughes, Raytheon, and RCA pleaded guilty to illegal trafficking in classified documents and paid a total of almost $15 million in restitution, reimbursements, fines, etc.

* Hughes pleaded guilty to procurement fraud in one case, was convicted of it in a second case, and, along with McDonnell Douglas and General Motors, settled out of court for a total of more than $1 million in a third case.

* Teledyne paid $5 million in a civil settlement for false testing, plus $5 million for repairs.

* McDonnell Douglas settled for a total of more than $22 million in four "defective pricing" cases.

But General Electric was the champ. PGO lists fourteen cases, including a conviction for mail and procurement fraud that resulted in a criminal fine of $10 million and restitution of $2.2 million. In our own research, we found several other examples of GE crimes and civil violations:

* In 1961, GE pleaded guilty to price-fixing and paid a $372,500 fine.

* In 1977, it was convicted of price-fixing again.

* In 1979, it settled out of court when the state of Alabama sued it for dumping PCBs in a river.

* In 1981, it was convicted of setting up a $1.25 million slush fund to bribe Puerto Rican officials.

* In 1985, GE pleaded guilty to 108 counts of fraud on a Minuteman missile contract. In addition, the chief engineer of GE's space systems division was convicted of perjury, and GE paid a fine of a million dollars.

* In 1985, it pleaded guilty to falsifying time cards.

* In 1989, it paid the government $3.5 million to settle five civil lawsuits alleging contractor fraud at a jet-engine plant (which involved the alteration of nine thousand daily labor vouchers to inflate its Pentagon billings).

In 1990, GE was convicted of criminal fraud for cheating the army on a contract for battlefield computers; it declined to appeal and paid $16 million in criminal and civil fines. (Of this amount, $11.7 million was to settle government complaints that it had padded its bids on two hundred other military and space contracts which comes to just $58,000 or so per contract.)

In 1993, GE sold its weapons division to Martin Marietta for $3 billion (retaining 23.5 percent of the stock and two seats on the board of directors).

The largest investigation of Pentagon fraud took place between 1986 and 1990. Called Operation Ill Wind, it began when Pentagon official John Marlowe was caught molesting little girls. He cut a deal to stay out of jail and, for the next few years, secretly recorded hundreds of conversations with weapons contractors.

There's no way of knowing how much the crimes Ill Wind looked into cost the taxpayers, but the investigation cost $20 million and brought in ten times that much in fines. According to *Wall Street Journal* reporter Andy Pasztor, "More than 90 companies and individuals were convicted of felonies...including eight of the military's fifteen largest suppliers....Boeing, GE and United Technologies pleaded guilty...Hughes, Unisys, Raytheon, Loral,

Litton, Teledyne, Cubic, Hazeltine, Whittaker and LTV...admitted they violated the law."

Unisys signed the largest Pentagon fraud settlement in history: $190 million in fines, penalties, and forgone profits (which means *for over 42* it wasn't allowed to charge for cost overruns the way military contractors usually do).

Assistant Navy Secretary Melvyn Paisley was the central figure in the Ill Wind scandal and the highest-ranking person convicted (he was sentenced to four years in prison). He ran his office like a supermarket for weapons manufacturers, soaking up bribes, divvying up multibillion-dollar contracts, **and diverting work to a firm he secretly controlled with a partner.**

Paisley may have been a bit more...flamboyant than most, but there was nothing terribly unusual about his approach. As of 1994, nearly seventy of the Pentagon's one hundred largest suppliers were under investigation. Fines for that year totaled a record $1.2 billion.

That may sound like a lot, but it's less than 2 percent of the weapons industry's net income (which averaged $64 billion a year in 1994 and 1995). A billion or two in fines is hardly an incentive to end the corruption and waste in Pentagon contracting.

PART – 6

GOVERNMENT ENTITLEMENTS
ARE KILLING US

A new Cato Policy Analysis examines so-called "entitlement programs" – chiefly Social Security, Medicare, and Medicaid – and how they will push the government's finances to the brink if they're not reined in. As he notes in the introduction, if politicians continue to duck the issue, they "will condemn our children and our grandchildren to a world of mounting debt and higher taxes."

The vast majority of future debt is driven neither by defense nor discretionary programs but by so-called entitlement programs, three in particular: Social Security, Medicare, and Medicaid. In fact, by 2050, those three programs alone are expected to consume every penny that the federal government raises in taxes. That means that everything else that the government does, from domestic programs to national defense, including paying interest on the federal debt, will have to be paid for through still more debt, or else government will have to raise taxes to astronomical levels. As the full burden of entitlement programs kicks in, the federal government will consume more than 40 percent of

GDP by the middle of the century. Again, half of that will be for Social Security, Medicare, and Medicaid.

Some thoughts from great men;

The Federal Government is not supposed to be some kind of a drive-through social services agency where every State and any individual can just drive in, roll down their window, and simply load up with all kinds of Federal freebies." – Scott Rohter.

"The nearest thing to eternal life on earth is a government program." – President Ronald Reagan.

The fox needs to kill its prey in order to survive, and the U.S. Federal Government thinks that it needs to pass more laws and exercise more control over its citizens in order for it to continue to be relevant in their lives. To remain relevant in the lives of millions of Americans is the same thing for the US Government as survival is for the fox! But it is actually even worse than that, because the Federal Government actually does need to pass more laws and exercise more control over its American victims, in order for millions of government employees to continue to have jobs! – President Ronald Reagan.

Actually, all government programs do one thing very well. They control their victims! When reduced to their basics, government programs control victims: victims of poverty, victims of unemployment, victims of natural disasters, victims of crime, and finally victims of our own Federal Government itself, which actually should be a crime! But in the end, all government programs turn us into victims! We are all turned into victims by the enabling hand of the Federal Government! – President Herbert Hoover.

U.S. households are getting more financial assistance from the federal government than ever before. Data from the 2011 U.S. Census Bureau shows that 49.1 percent of U.S. Households are now receiving some sort of federal benefits, according to the *Wall Street Journal*.

Those numbers are up dramatically from the early 1980s, when just 30 percent of households received the same benefits, and up from 44.4 percent in the third quarter of 2008. Broken down by benefit, at least one person enrolled in Medicaid per household in 26 percent of American homes, one person is receiving Social Security in 16 percent, at least one person is receiving some sort of unemployment benefits in 2 percent and at least one person is on food stamps in 15 percent. At this rate, by 2014 when Obama's new health entitlement system kicks in, more Americans than not will be receiving government assistance for the first time in U.S. history.

For at least a decade, under both President Clinton and President Bush, as well as President Obama, experts inside and outside government have made it clear that entitlement reform was essential to the nation's long-term fiscal health. Most recently, in December 2010, the bipartisan Commission on Fiscal Responsibility and Reform warned that we have reached a "moment of truth" than the $14.3 trillion currently authorized. But our current budget problems are nothing compared to the explosion to come. The Congressional Budget Office predicts that the official debt alone (excluding the unfunded liabilities of entitlement programs) will exceed 100 percent of GDP by 2025 and could exceed No area of government spending has been immune from this explosion of spending. Since 2000, domestic discretionary spending has increased by 120 percent, and defense spending has risen by 135 percent. Both defense and domestic spending will have to be reduced if we are to begin putting our fiscal house in order. But the damage from big government should not be seen in strictly economic terms. Much of what government does actually does more harm than good. Government social welfare programs, for instance, encourage dependency, discourage work-effort, and create disincentives for family formation. Government retirement programs crowd out private savings and can leave retirees with lower levels of retirement benefits than they might have.

All this entitlement spending has punched a hole in the government budget and ballooned the federal deficit to dizzying heights.

The depth of the budget problem was underscored last week, when the Treasury reported that the government ran a $1.26 trillion deficit for the first 11 months of the fiscal year, on pace to be the second-biggest on record.

And the future looks even worse. For the period from 2011 to 2020, the Congressional Budget Office (CBO) forecasts a budget deficit of $6.047 trillion, while the Obama administration projects a shortfall of $8.532 trillion.

The lowest projected deficit in the next decade is a $706 billion shortfall forecast for the fiscal year that ends in September 2014. That doesn't sound too bad in the context of the 2009 -2011 figures, but it's almost $300 billion larger than the highest federal-budget deficit in human history before 2009.

But generally speaking, too many Americans feel entitled to all kinds of government largess. It has driven up deficits and debt, and it's sapping the nation's competitive and creative energies.

Just how bad has it got? Since 1970, means-tested entitlements in America have increased -- ready -- An 150 million Americans live in households that receive some kind of government assistance. It's almost half the population.

Social justice, the primary reason the USA is changing into an entitlement country much like the western European nations.

Politicians in both parties understand that giving money away means votes. Also there is no question that both the feds and the states have loosened standards under which Americans receive entitlements. Since President Obama has been in office, federal welfare spending is up about 41 percent. Food stamps up about 135 percent since 2007; from 30 billion to 72 billion a year; disability payments up 116 percent from a decade ago. More than three million American workers have signed up for disability since President Obama took office.

It's pervasive. It's seen everywhere from grade schools, where every kid is a winner and no one loses, to the federal home-lending programs that required only marginal ability to repay the mortgage and led to the collapse of the housing markets across the country.

The growing acceptance of entitlements reflects a shift in American cultural attitudes. Those who survived the Depression, although they got help from the New Deal, did not expect a handout. They always looked first to their own hands for assistance. Those days and experiences are gone, and no one wants to relive that time. Modern

Americans should, however, hold on to some of that tested moral fiber and self-sufficient economic determinism.

John F. Kennedy, in his inaugural address had it right: "My fellow Americans, ask not what your country can do for you -- ask what you can do for your country." And, he followed with, "My fellow citizens of the world, ask not what America will do for you, but what together we can do for the freedom of man." He had it right when he said: "It's not what your country can do for you, it's what you can do for your country."

In the last five chapters I have exposed many areas of outrageous waste and fraud of our tax dollars in our government. But what I have to say at this point may be hard for some of you to accept or understand.

All of the blame cannot be just place on the shoulders of our politicians. For we as a nation who have become a nation of sheep are also to blame. We need to change our paradigm. We need to change our thought process of "What is in it for me" to "What can we do". We need to take a proactive roll in establishing the guidelines in which the country is run. Rather than being told by government how it is going to be. Until we unite together with a common goal and singular direction to head. We will always be subjected to being lead like sheep.

PART – 7

"TAXATION WITHOUT REPRESENTATION"

One of the world's more pressing problems is sovereign debt. From Japan to Greece to America, the debts run up by governments are forcing painful choices.

But some think we needn't make hard choices. They think things can go on as before and that government can take on even more debt and start up even more public programs. Some are unwilling to make any sacrifices; they don't want to give up anything.

In America as in Europe, those most averse to change are government employees. The evidence for this has been seen recently in states trying to get control of their deficits. A prime example is Wisconsin, where protesting government employees; teachers, students, unionists, and a few anarchists occupied the state Capitol for weeks.

The big issue for state employees in Wisconsin was the loss of collective bargaining. Wisconsin needed to scale back collective bargaining so that it can control runaway benefit costs and so that bad employees can be fired without incurring huge legal bills. States wanting to cut their deficits must address spending; they can't just raise taxes, as residents and businesses will decamp for other states.

To see what the states are up against, watch the video of filmmaker Michael Moore on March 5 in Madison, where he delivered a speech to thousands of protesters, inflaming their passions and class resentments, telling them that America is "awash" in cash "It's just that it's not in your hands."

The cost of personnel is one of the biggest expenses for a state (or for any enterprise). If a state can't control what it pays for employees, it's unlikely to get control of its budget. In his April 1 article "We've Become a Nation of Takers, Not Makers" for the *Wall Street Journal*, Stephen Moore relates that the annual cost of employees to state and local governments is $1 trillion, almost half their budgets. Here's more Moore:

If you want to understand better why so many states—from New York to Wisconsin to California—are teetering on the brink of bankruptcy, consider this depressing statistic: Today in America there are nearly twice as many people working for the government (22.5 million) than in all of manufacturing (11.5 million). This is an almost exact reversal of the situation in 1960, when there were fifteen million workers in manufacturing and 8.7 million collecting a paycheck from the government.

The mushrooming number of government employees isn't the only problem, however; government employees have higher average compensation than private sector workers. Some contend that this is false. But a recent study from the Heritage Foundation by Jason Richwine and Andrew Biggs confirms it. And on April 4 in a related article at NRO, they write:

Sadly, it's easier to put out a dozen poor studies than to get a single analysis right. But many fights on public sector pay are yet to come in states around the country. Taxpayers and their advocates need to be ready to counter false claims about government pay.

The dollar impact of employee costs on government deficits isn't the only issue—there's the issue of equity:

Borrowing money to pay for current government spending involves deferred taxation. And when elected officials make contracts with unions to pay for open-ended pensions and benefits, they are again kicking taxation off to the future. The problem is that one of the parties to these decisions—the party that will fulfill such government promises was not represented: the future taxpayer. So deficit spending and open-ended benefits for government employees are a form of "taxation without representation."

In postponing taxation, politicians make a claim on the earnings of the future taxpayer for the purpose of handing out free goodies to the current taxpayer. Government contracts with government employees should extend only for the term of those officials approving such contracts, or two years. The next electorate may vote in officials who wouldn't sign such agreements. This is why "defined benefit" pensions have got to go. Such pensions are fair for neither the future taxpayer or for the public employees who may lose their pensions. Better to own your pension than to rely on the willingness of future taxpayers to fulfill promises to which they didn't agree. Better to take the money and run.

If it is true that no Congress can bind a future Congress, then how can any Congress bind a future electorate or the future taxpayer? For that matter, how binding is any contract made for someone who didn't agree to it? Not even Congress should presume to sign agreements that others must fulfill except for the voters who gave them power.

If current taxpayers are unwilling to pay the price for current government, then scale back current spending. But don't make future generations into tax slaves.

Change may be OK for the rest of America, but not for government employees. They don't appreciate the gravity of the sovereign debt crisis, or that bankruptcy looms, or that ruin is at hand. If money is short, that's your problem.

So as The Judge so elegantly puts it on "Freedom Watch," "Does the government work for us, or do we work for the government?"

At a time when workers' pay and benefits have stagnated, federal employees' average compensation has grown to more than double what private sector workers earn, a *USA Today* analysis finds.

Federal workers have been awarded bigger average pay and benefit increases than private employees for nine years in a row. The compensation gap between federal and private workers has doubled in the past decade.

Federal civil servants earned average pay and benefits of $123,049 in 2009 while private workers made $61,051 in total compensation, according to the Bureau of Economic Analysis. The data are the latest available.

The federal compensation advantage has grown from $30,415 in 2000 to $61,998 last year.

Public employee unions say the compensation gap reflects the increasingly high level of skill and education required for most federal jobs and the government contracting out lower-paid jobs to the private sector in recent years.

"The data are not useful for a direct public-private pay comparison," says Colleen Kelley, president of the National Treasury Employees Union.

Chris Edwards, a budget analyst at the libertarian Cato Institute, thinks otherwise. "Can't we now all agree that federal workers are overpaid and do something about it?" he asks.

Last week, President Obama ordered a freeze on bonuses for 2,900 political appointees. For the rest of the two million-person federal workforce, Obama asked for a 1.4 percent across-the-board pay hike in 2011, the smallest in more than a decade. Federal workers also would qualify for seniority pay hikes.

Congressional Republicans want to cancel the across-the-board increase in 2011, which would save $2.2 billion.

"Americans are fed up with public employee pay scales far exceeding that in the private sector," says Representative Eric Cantor (R-VA), the second-ranking Republican in the House.

Senator Ted Kaufman (D-DE) says a pay freeze would unfairly scapegoat federal workers without addressing real budget problems.

What the data show:

•Benefits. Federal workers received average benefits worth $41,791 in 2009. Most of this was the government's contribution to pensions. Employees contributed an additional $10,569.

•Pay. The average federal salary has grown 33 percent faster than inflation since 2000. *USA Today* reported in March that the federal government pays an average of 20 percent more than private firms for comparable occupations. The analysis did not consider differences in experience and education.

•Total compensation. Federal compensation has grown 36.9 percent since 2000 after adjusting for inflation, compared with 8.8 percent for private workers.

PART – 8

DO YOU HAVE A SPECIAL INTEREST?

According to a study by the Center for Responsive Politics, special interests paid Washington lobbyists $3.2 billion in 2008—more than any other year on record. This was a 13.7 percent increase from 2007 (which broke the record by 7.7 percent over 2006).

The center calculates that interest groups spent $17.4 million on lobbying for every day Congress was in session in 2008, or $32,523 per legislator per day. Center director Sheila Krumholz says, "The federal government is handing out billions of dollars by the day, and that translates into job security for lobbyists who can help companies and industries get a piece of the payout."

Health interests spent more on federal lobbying than any other economic sector. Their $478.5 million guaranteed the crown for the third year, with the finance, insurance, real estate sector a runner-up, spending $453.5 million. The pharmaceutical/health products industry contributed $230.9 million, raising its past eleven-year total to over $1.6 billion. The second-biggest spender among industries in 2008 was electric utilities, which spent $156.7 million on lobbying, followed by insurance, which spent $153.2 million, and oil and gas, which paid lobbyists $133.2 million. Pro-Israel groups, food processing companies, and the oil and gas industry increased their lobbying expenditures the most (as a percentage) between 2007 and 2008.

Finance, insurance, and real estate companies have been competing to get a piece of the $700 billion bailout package Congress approved late last year. The companies that reduced lobbying the most are those that declared bankruptcy or were taken over by the federal government and stopped their lobbying operations altogether. "Even though some financial, insurance, and real estate interests pulled back last year, they still managed to spend more than $450 million as a sector to lobby policy makers. That can buy a lot of influence, and it's a fraction of what the financial sector is reaping in return through the government's bailout program," Krumholz said.

Business and real estate associations and coalitions were among the organizations that ramped up their lobbying expenditures the most last year. The National Association of Realtors increased spending by 25 percent, from $13.9 million to $17.3 million. The American Bankers Association spent $9.1 million in 2008, a 47 percent increase from 2007. Other industry groups that spent more in 2008 include the Private Equity Council, the Mortgage Bankers Association of America, and the Financial Services Roundtable.

The US Chamber of Commerce remained the number one spender on lobbying in 2008, spending nearly $92 million—more than

$350,000 every weekday, and a 73 percent increase over 2007—to advocate for its members' interests. Pro-business associations as a whole increased their lobbying 47 percent between 2007 and 2008.

With record spending on lobbying, some industries face serious cutbacks and have put the brakes on spending, but they have not discontinued the practice. Automotive companies decreased the amount they paid lobbyists by 7.6 percent, from $70.9 million to $65.5 million. This is a big change from prior years; auto manufacturers and dealers increased lobbying spending by 21 percent between 2006 and 2007. Between 2007 and 2008 the Alliance of Automobile Manufacturers, which testified before Congress with Detroit's Big Three last year, decreased its reported lobbying by 43 percent, from $12.8 million to $7.3 million. Of the Big Three, only one company, Ford, increased its efforts, though not by much: It went from $7.1 million to $7.7 million, an 8 percent increase.

Among Washington lobbying firms, Patton Boggs reported the highest revenues from registered lobbying for the fifth year in a row: 41.9 million dollars, an increase over 2006 of more than 20 percent. The firm's most lucrative clients included private equity firm Cerberus Capital Management, confection and pet food maker Mars, communication provider Verizon, pharmaceutical manufacturers Bristol-Myers Squibb and Roche, and the American Association for Justice (formerly the Association of Trial Lawyers of America).

It seems as if this should be a classified ad: "Laid off and looking for work? The lobbying industry wants you!" Since we posted this story on OpenSecrets.org in January, the lobbying industry has only continued to grow, even as industries across the board have continued to shrink, forcing hundreds of thousands of Americans out of work. This growth could be attributed in part to the economy itself—many executives are looking for some help from the government to keep their businesses afloat. Others are simply taking advantage of the opportunities that a spate of government handouts has presented. But as long as there's a federal government calling the shots, lobbyists will be paid more and more each year to hold their clients' fire to lawmakers' feet.

Year after year we see increases in lobbying expenditures—in fact, 100 percent over the past decade—and the flurry of activity during the first three months of 2009 indicates that the trend won't come to an end any time soon. Based on records from the Senate Office of Public Records, the nonpartisan Center for Responsive Politics found that from January through March, lobbying increased slightly compared *for over 42* with the same period of time last year, by at least $2.4 million. Unions, organizations, and companies spent at least $799.7 million so far this year on sending influence peddlers to Capitol Hill, compared with $797.2 million during the same time in 2008. That might seem like a small increase compared with the billions spent each year on this activity, but in a time of economic turmoil, that's a hefty revenue stream for a single industry.

That said, the industries that have made the most headlines for the help they've asked for or received from the federal government actually decreased the amount they spent on lobbying in the first three months of 2009 compared with 2008. Recipients of cash from the federal government's Troubled Asset Relief Program (TARP) handed out less money to lobbyists than they had in any quarter of 2008, in part, perhaps, because they faced new rules restricting their lobbying contact with officials in connection with the bailout program. CRP found that TARP recipients have spent $13.9

million on lobbying so far this year, compared with $20.2 million in January through March of last year and $17.8 million in the last three months of 2008. With the government doling out billions of dollars, these sums pale in comparison with the benefit the companies are reaping.

Now, whom do you have to speak on your behalf in Washington?

Is it not time we change this?

PART - 9

PARTING THOUGHTS AND FUTURE REVIEWS

Now I feel that I have given you enough information to feed on to make a decision. Are you happy with the status quo or do you truly want to do something about the state of our Country?

My next informational booklet will outline just what actions can be taken by all of us to initiate a change in the direction of our Government.

Here are twelve examples for Topics of discussion:

Strict Term Limits on our Congress and House of Representatives.

All Congress and House of Representatives pay increases will be voted on by the people of this Nation and not by themselves.

Line Item Veto for all Presidents to eliminate special interest groups from wasting tax payers money on frivolous items.

Elimination of non-essential departments within the Government. Ex.U. S. Postal Service (Privatize with the times)

TSA (Privatize)

Excessive Government Agencies and employees (To date there are over 1,300 Federal Agencies. Many are redundant and outright useless. Ex. Obama Health Care Bill created 159 new Commissions and Boards just to manage the program.)

Drastically reduce the amount of financial support given to foreign nations.

Government Entitlements (programs); in 2005 there were over 1,607 Entitlement programs costing our nation over 1.9 TRILLION dollars.

Government Entitlements(programs) in 2012; The larges beneficiaries to the program are all allocated to the top four Government programs like, Government Defense, Government Health Care, Government Education and Welfare costing the American public over 6.3 Trillion dollars. With Obama's plan the same programs will exceed 10.3 trillion in the next ten years.

Defense Budget; If you add up all the money spent on military systems that got funded but not fielded since the Cold War ended, it probably tops $100 billion. We'll never know the full amount, because some of the biggest projects are hidden in secret spy-agency accounts. Defense contractors are reflexively blamed for the waste because politicians and policymakers are even less interested in accountability than they are in precise accounting.

NASA Space Agency: In it's latest adventure to Mars, it cost the tax payers 2.2 Billion dollars. And its design purpose is to Check for Carbon, Radiation, Water and Carbon Dioxide. Think about what this money could have done to find the cure for Diabetes. This has been identified as one of the main reasons of escalating Health Care Costs in America.

Department of Energy (DOE) Does anybody remember the reason given for the establishment of the DEPARTMENT OF ENERGY during the Carter Administration?

Bottom line: We've spent several hundred billion dollars in support of an agency....the reason for which possibly not one person who reads this can remember! It was very simple...and at the time, everybody thought it very appropriate.

The Department of Energy was instituted on 8/04/1977, "To Lessen Our Dependency On Foreign Oil". And now it's 2012 --- 35 years later, and the budget for this so called "Necessary" department is at 27.2 billion for the fiscal year 2013. "That's correct, 27.2 BILLION dollars. It has over 16,000 employees and approximately 100,000 contract employees. And look at the job it has done!

35 years ago 30% of our oil consumption was foreign imports. Today less than 50% of our oil consumption is foreign imports.

Now we have rolled over and turned over the banking system, health care, and education guidelines of our children to the same government!

Once again quietly, we go like sheep to slaughter.

Establish a truly aggressive campaign for Energy Self Reliance in our country. We need to stop suckling on the nipple of Middle Eastern countries and become self-sufficient.

Set a Maximum, for the amount of money to be spent on all elections. We will no longer accept the richest person to be the only contender. Ex. Barack Obama's presidential campaign shattered all records by raising $760 million in his first election cycle. That record is not likely to last much longer — President Obama and Presidential Candidate Romney are expected to raise more than $1 billion each for their re-election and election campaign. And overall spending by all candidates in 2012 is predicted to eclipse an astounding $8 billion.

Are you ready to take back our Country? I will be talking to you again soon to discuss just how you can stand up and be counted as an active participant in the true change in the United States of America and no longer be looked at as passive sheep by the self-proclaimed elite of Washington DC.